Good Weather

Weather

The Acadiana Sampler Cookbook

Good Gumbo Weather
The Acadiana Sampler Cookbook

All Rights Reserved © 2011 by Todd-Michael St. Pierre

Cover Design and Art Work by Diane Millsap
www.neworleans-art.net

No part of this book may be reproduced or transmitted in an form or by any means, graphic, electronic, or mechanical, including photocopying, recording, taping, or by any information storage or retrieval system, without the permission in writing from the publisher.

Pontchartrain Press
New Orleans, Louisiana

For Information
www.louisianaboy.com

ISBN: 144213996X

Preface

Any time's a good time for gumbo, be it seafood, with shrimp, crabs, crawfish & oysters, or how about chicken & andouille or even turkey neck. With okra or with filé... with spicy smoked sausage, wild game or tasso... & don't forget your trinity (onion, celery, & bell pepper) or The Pope (garlic)! The possibilities are endless!

Gumbo is so much more than mere sustenance in south Louisiana, it's a ritual that brings people together, where we share our heritage, our music, our pride & our memories! We remain faithful, we bounce back... but most of all we make gumbo & we share it! Because it's who we are!

This new collection of Cajun favorites will guide you through all things Gumbo & beyond! First cool snap? Warm January? Chilly April? Raining cats & dogs? Rare sneauxfall? Hurricane blowing?

Here in the Bayou State, no matter the forecast, it's always...

Good Gumbo Weather!

WWW.LOUISIANABOY.COM

Dedication

In memory of my Maw-Maw Dorothy...the best gumbo cook I've ever known.

Love,

Todd-Michael

And also in honor of my Acadian heritage (LeBlanc and Thibodeaux).

Table of Contents

And First You Make a Roux..1
   Dry Roux.. 2
   Roux... 4
Raised on Gumbeaux 7
   Kaliste Saloom Seafood gumbo............................8
   Carencro Shrimp, Crab & Okra Gumbo...............10
   Henderson Scallop Gumbo..................................12
   Galliano Gumbo Degas..14
   Gueydan Gumbo with Okra & Stewed Tomatoes! 16
   Patterson Seafood Gumbo...................................18
   Gramercy Crawfish Gumbo..................................20
   Fleur-de-Lisa's Low Calorie Rabbit and Chicken Sausage Gumbo... 22
   Jeanerette Seafood and Turkey-Sausage Gumbo 24
   Abbeville Shrimp and Egg Gumbo........................28
   Mon Mere's Gumbo..30
   Bunkie Chicken and Andouille Gumbo.................33
Salades Satisfaisante..37
   Arceneaux's Artichoke Salad 38
   Lake Martin Crawfish and Egg Salad 39
   T-Coon's Cajun Potato Salad...............................40
   Fontenot's Fried Oyster Salad..............................41
   Blanchard Beet Salad..42
   St. Mary's Strawberry Fields Forever Salad.........44

Bisques, Soupes and Stews..................................47
   Bertrand's Corn Bisque with Crabmeat...............48
   Vita's Vegetable Soup...50
   Lafourche Parish White Bean Soup......................51
   Terrebonne Oyster Soup..52
   Trahan Oyster and Artichoke Soup......................54
   Cecelia Sweet Corn And Shrim Soup...................56
   Breaux Bridge Crawfish Stew................................58
   Kaplan Chicken Stew!..60
   Theriot Tomato Basil Soup....................................61
Accoutrements...63
   Eunice Dirty Rice...64
   Duplechain Dirty Rice..66
   Mowata Couche Couche..67
   Trosclair Cornbread and Andouille Sausage
   Stuffing.. 68
   Chenevert Mirliton & Crawfish Casserole...........70
   Cottonport Crawfish Casserole............................ 72
   Latiolais Maque Choux..73
   Bourgeois Crawfish Pasta Casserole...................74
   Cameron Mirliton Dressing...................................76
   Big Pete's Fried Cauliflower..................................78
   Atchafalaya Cheese Straws..................................80
   Jennings Tomato Gravy...81
A Lotta Lagniappe..83
   Cocodrie Cracklin...84
   Parrain Pete's Boiled Cajun Peanuts...................85
   New Iberia Crawfish Boudin 86
   Ville Platte Seafood Linguine................................87

Landry Crawfish Etouffee 88
Charington Shrimp Creole 90
Opelousas Jambalaya 92
Gonzales Jambalaya 94
Thibodaux Crawfish & Tasso Jambalaya 96
Guidry's Deep-Fried Turkey 98
Broussard Fried Oysters 99
LeBlanc's Shrimp-Stuffed Mirlitons 100
Jeansonne Crawfish Pie 102
St. Amant Cajun Meatloaf 104
Big Peter's Boiled Crawfish 106
Clotilde's Cajun Cornish Hens 108
Lacassine Peppered Shrimp 109
Lake Charles Cajun Pizza 110
La Dent Sucree 113
   Rayne Strawberries and Cream Bread Pudding. 114
   Baleu's Banana Nut Muffins 115
   Assumption Parish Beignets 116
   Louisiana Watermelon Cake 118
   Granier Red velvet cupcakes 120
   St. Martinville Peach Cobbler 122
   LA Louisiane Smooth Pecan Pralines 124
   Purgatory Pie 125
About the Author 126

And First You Make a Roux...

Dry Roux

A great way to make gumbo lighter in calories is to use a dry roux. This is made with no oil which results in less fat content and is a boon to lovers of gumbo who must be careful of fat intake. It is easy to make, stores well and makes an authentic Louisiana gumbo.

Skillet Roux

Directions

1. Place 1-2 cups of flour in a large heavy pot or a deep iron skillet on medium heat and stir constantly for 15 to 20 minutes.
2. Continue stirring until close to the color of peanut butter or pecans. It must be a lighter color than a standard version made with oil. The lighter color will result in a dark gumbo.
3. Store in a glass jar or plastic container.
4. For larger quantities this can be done in an oven.

Oven Baked Roux

Directions

1. Place 3-4 cups flour in a big iron skillet or heavy dutch oven.
2. Put in a 400°F oven and cook for 45 minutes to 1 hour. Depending on your individual oven the cooking time may be more or it could be less.
3. Stir at 10 minute intervals.
4. When it reaches an evenly browned peanut butter color remove and let cool.
5. Store in a jar or plastic container.

Roux

Ingredients

- 1 cup of vegetable oil
- 1 cup of flour

Directions

1. Heat a heavy skillet on a low to medium setting.
2. Add the oil and allow it to heat.
3. Slowly add the flour while constantly stirring it.
4. The longer you cook the roux, the darker it will get. Take care not to burn it.

Raised on Gumbeaux

Kaliste Saloom Seafood gumbo

Ingredients

- 1½ sticks salted butter
- Large onion
- 4-5 green onions
- 1-2 teaspoon minced garlic
- Large bell pepper
- One celery stalk
- 3-4 carrots
- 4-5 medium white potatoes
- ½ cup flour
- 2 (14.5 oz) cans chicken broth
- 1 (12 oz) can evaporated milk
- 1 quart Half and Half
- 1 can cream corn
- 2 cans corn
- 1½ pounds Louisiana crawfish
- 1 pound crabmeat
- Seasoning to taste

Directions

1. Melt butter and sauté onions, green onions, garlic, bell pepper and celery for about 30 minutes.
2. Season to taste. Add flour and mix well.
3. Stir in one can broth, evaporated milk and half of the half and half.
4. Dice carrots and potatoes and add to mixture.
5. Cook for 45 minutes, stirring often and adding broth and half and half as needed.
6. Add all cans of corn (un-drained) and cook an additional 30 minutes.
7. Add crawfish, lower heat to medium and cook an additional 10 minutes.
8. Stir in crab meat, and cook an additional 10-15 minutes.

Carencro Shrimp, Crab & Okra Gumbo

Ingredients

- ¼ cup dry roux
- 1 tablespoon canola oil
- 1 cup chopped onion
- 1 cup chopped green bell pepper
- 3 garlic cloves, chopped
- 1 cup sliced okra
- 1 bay leaf
- 1 cup low-salt seafood or fish bouillon
- 2 teaspoons Creole or Cajun seasoning
- 16 uncooked large shrimp, peeled, deveined
- 8 ounces jumbo lump crab meat

Directions

1. Heat oil in same pot over medium heat.
2. Add onion and bell pepper and sauté until tender.
3. Add garlic and bay leaf.
4. Add browned flour.
5. Add bouillon and seasoning.
6. Bring to boil.
7. Reduce heat, cover and simmer 20 minutes to blend flavors, stirring frequently.
8. Add Shrimp to pot and simmer just until seafood is opaque in center.
9. Discard bay leaf.
10. Turn off heat and add lump crab to pot. Let stand for 5 minute.
11. Season with salt and pepper.
12. Serve over rice and add filé.

Henderson Scallop Gumbo

Ingredients

- ¼ cup olive oil
- 2 tablespoons butter
- ⅓ cup flour
- onion, chopped
- 1 green bell pepper, chopped
- celery stalks, chopped
- tablespoons minced garlic
- 1 teaspoon salt
- ¼ teaspoon black pepper
- 2½ cups chicken stock, unsalted
- 2 cups tomatoes, chopped
- 1 tablespoon fresh thyme
- 1 tablespoon fresh oregano
- 1 tablespoon bay leaf
- 1 Cayenne to taste
- 1 pound scallops
- ½ cup parsley, fresh, chopped

Directions

1. Put oil and butter in a large pot or Dutch oven over medium-low heat.
2. When butter is melted, add flour and cook, stirring almost constantly,
3. until roux darkens and becomes fragrant, about 15 to 20 minutes; as it
4. cooks, adjust heat as necessary to keep mixture from burning.
5. Add onion, bell pepper, celery and garlic and raise heat to medium.
6. Sprinkle with salt and pepper and cook, stirring frequently, until
7. vegetables have softened, about 10 more minutes.
8. Stir in the stock, tomatoes, thyme, oregano, bay leaves and cayenne.
9. Cover, bring to a boil, then reduce heat so soup bubbles steadily.
10. Cook for about 20 minutes or until flavors meld.
11. Add scallops and cook until they are no longer translucent, about 2minutes.
12. Remove bay leaves.
13. Taste, adjust seasoning and serve, garnished with parsley.

Galliano Gumbo Degas

Ingredients

- 4 pounds. shrimp
- 2 pounds okra
- ½ cup flour
- 3 large. onions
- 1 cup parsley
- 1 cup yellow bell pepper
- 1 bay leaf
- 1 teaspoon thyme
- ½ teaspoon garlic puree
- 1 teaspoon white pepper
- ½ teaspoon paprika
- 1 pinch allspice
- 1 tablespoon Worcestershire
- ½ teaspoon cayenne pepper
- 1 cup olive oil
- 2 quart shrimp water*
- 1 dozen gumbo crabs
- 1 12-ounce can peeled tomatoes
- 2 tablespoon salt

Directions

1. Fry okra in flour and olive oil, then fry onion and add rest of spices, yellow bell pepper, parsley, etc.
2. Cook ½ hour then add tomatoes and cook additional ½ hour.
3. Add shrimp water and crabs.
4. Cook until done to taste.
5. Serve in large shallow soup bowl over fresh cooked rice.

*Shrimp Water

1. After peeling shrimp, boil the peelings and heads in 2 quarts water.
2. Add water while boiling to maintain 2 quart level.

Gueydan Gumbo with Okra & Stewed Tomatoes!

Ingredients

- 3 tablespoons corn oil
- 1 cup flour
- 1 cup yellow onion, minced
- ¼ cup parsley, minced
- ¼ cup garlic, minced
- ¼ cup yellow bell pepper, chopped
- 1 can stewed tomatoes
- ¾ cup chopped okra
- ¼ cup celery leaves, minced
- 2 cups crawfish tails, cleaned
- 1 cup crabmeat
- 8 cups of water
- ¼ cup sherry
- 3 teaspoons Cajun & Creole seasoning to taste

Directions

1. Make your roux (pronounced rew).
2. Heat oven to 350°F.
3. Place flour in a 9-inch pie plate.
4. Bake for 45 minutes or until browned, stirring occasionally.
   Roux should be dark brown in this case.
5. Next add onions and cook for 3-4 minutes or until onions are soft.
6. Continue stirring while cooking over low heat until oil floats on top.
7. Add water, parsley, garlic, okra, stewed tomatoes, celery leaves, bell pepper & Cajun & Creole seasoning.
8. Simmer over low heat for 1 hour.
9. Add crawfish tails, crabmeat and sherry.
   Let simmer for 25 additional minutes.
   Just before serving, add 3/4 teaspoon filé powder, (pronounced fee-lay) if desired.
10. Serve in bowls over a scoop of hot steamed brown rice and drizzle with a few of drops of Louisiana Hot Sauce!
11. Garnish center of gumbo with fresh parsley.

   I love freshly baked French bread with mine!

Patterson Seafood Gumbo

Ingredients

- 1 teaspoon canola oil
- 1 cup dry roux
- 4 cups, fat-free chicken broth
- 1 cup chopped celery
- 2 onions, chopped
- 1 pound shrimp
- 2 cans chopped tomatoes
- 10 ounce package frozen, chopped okra
- 1 teaspoon Tabasco sauce
- 2 cups crab meat
- 1 pound low-fat smoked sausage, diced
- 1 teaspoon oregano
- ½ teaspoon black pepper
- 1 teaspoon Cajun seasoning
- 1 teaspoon garlic powder
- 2 tablespoons Worcestershire Sauce
- 4 cups cooked rice

Directions

1. Add 1 cup dry roux and 1 chicken broth.
2. Add celery, onion, okra and smoked sausage.
3. Cook over medium heat, stirring constantly, until vegetables are tender.
4. Add 3 cups chicken broth, tomatoes, Worcestershire sauce, Tabasco, pepper, garlic powder, oregano, and Cajun seasoning.
5. Cook over medium heat for 30 minutes.
6. Add shrimp and crab meat.
7. Cook another 20 minutes.
8. Serve over cooked rice.

Gramercy Crawfish Gumbo

Traditionally gumbo starts with a roux - a mixture of flour and fat that's cooked slowly until browned. In this recipe, named for a small town in Louisiana, you brown the flour in the oven. This technique provides a deep, nutty flavor without the fat.

Ingredients

- ½ cup all-purpose flour
- ¼ cup vegetable oil
- 1 cup finely chopped onion
- 8 cups water
- 1½ cups sliced okra pods (about 6 ounces)
- ¼ cup finely chopped green bell pepper
- ¼ cup chopped fresh parsley
- ¼ cup chopped celery leaves
- 2 to 3 tablespoons All That Jazz Seasoning
- 2 teaspoons salt
- 8 garlic cloves, minced
- 1 14.5-ounce can stewed tomatoes, undrained
- 2 cups cooked crawfish tail meat (about 12 ounces)
- 1 cup lump crabmeat, shell pieces removed (about 1/3 pound)
- 1 teaspoon hot sauce
- 6 cups hot cooked rice
- Chopped fresh parsley (optional)

Directions

1. Preheat oven to 350°F.

2. Lightly spoon flour into a dry measuring cup; level with a knife.
3. Place flour in a 9-inch pie plate; bake at 350° for 45 minutes or until lightly browned, stirring frequently.
4. Cool on a wire rack.
5. Heat oil in a large Dutch oven over medium-high heat.
6. Add onion and sauté 4 minutes.
7. Stir in browned flour and cook 1 minute, stirring constantly.
8. Gradually stir in water and next 8 ingredients (water through tomatoes).
9. Bring to a boil.
10. Reduce heat and simmer 1 hour.
11. Stir in crawfish, crabmeat, and hot sauce.
12. Bring to a boil; reduce heat, and simmer 25 minutes.
13. Serve gumbo with rice
14. Sprinkle with parsley, if desired.

Fleur-de-Lisa's Low Calorie Rabbit and Chicken Sausage Gumbo

Ingredients

- 1 tablespoon cooking oil
- 1 pound rabbit pieces (or deboned rabbit meat)
- 1 pound Smoked Chicken Sausage sliced or diced
- 1 cup chopped onions
- 1 cup chopped celery
- 1 cup chopped green pepper
- 3 cloves garlic diced
- 2 quarts chicken stock
- 1 ¼ teaspoon Creole seasoning (or ¾ teaspoon salt, ¼ teaspoon black pepper, ¼ teaspoon cayenne pepper, ½ teaspoon white pepper
- 1 bay leaf
- ½ cup dry roux
- ½ cup chopped green onions
- 2 tablespoons chopped parsley
- Hot cooked brown rice

Directions

1. In a large heavy pot heat the oil on high heat.
2. Add the rabbit and chicken sausage and cook for 10 minutes stirring constantly until brown.
3. Add the onions, celery, green pepper and garlic stirring until soft.
4. Add the stock, dry roux, seasonings and bay leaf, stir well and cook on low for 1 hour.
5. Stir occasionally to blend roux.
6. Add the green onions and parsley, cover and cook 5 more minutes.
7. Turn off heat and let stand for 5 minutes covered.
8. Serve with cooked brown rice.

This is great with your favorite potato salad and whole wheat french bread.

Jeanerette Seafood and Turkey-Sausage Gumbo

Here is a terrific lower-fat version of this classic dish.

Ingredients

- ¼ cup dry roux
- 1 tablespoon canola oil
- 1 cup chopped onion
- 1 cup chopped green bell pepper
- 3 garlic cloves, chopped
- 1 teaspoon dried thyme
- 1 bay leaf
- 3 low-fat turkey sausages (about 10 ounces)
- 1 28-ounce can diced tomatoes in juice
- 1 cup canned low-salt chicken broth or vegetable broth
- 2 teaspoons Creole or Cajun seasoning
- 8 uncooked large shrimp, peeled, deveined
- 2 6-ounce catfish fillets, each cut into 4 pieces

Directions

1. Heat oil in pot over medium heat.
2. Add onion and bell pepper and sauté until tender.
3. Add garlic, thyme and bay leaf; stir.
4. Add sausages and sauté until brown.
5. Add dry roux.

6. Add tomatoes with juices, broth and Creole seasoning.
7. Bring to boil.
8. Reduce heat, cover and simmer 20 minutes to blend flavors, stirring frequently.
9. Add shrimp and catfish to pot and simmer just until seafood is opaque in center, about 5 minutes.
10. Discard bay leaf.
11. Season with salt and pepper to taste.
12. Serve over rice.

CRAWFISH WATER

1. In a large 3-gallon stock pot fill with 2- gallons of water.
2. Place previously eaten crawfish heads (sounds gross to non-natives) and peelings in water. Bring to boil.
3. Add celery stalks, onions, carrots, garlic, bay leaf, thyme.
4. DO NOT add salt, pepper or any HOT seasonings. The seasoning from the crawfish heads and peelings will be MORE than sufficient!
5. Let simmer for at least an hour.
6. Strain and preserve the stock for future use.

May be frozen

Chackbay Crawfish, Okra & Andouille Gumbo

INGREDIENTS

- 1 pound Andouille sausage, half inch sliced
- cups okra, sliced
- 1 cup vegetable oil
- 1¼ cups flour
- cups onions, chopped
- 2 cups celery, chopped
- 1 cup bell pepper, chopped
- ¼ cup garlic, minced
- 1 quart crawfish stock (any seafood stock or a vegetable stock with a seafood "base" can be substituted)
- 2 pounds Louisiana crawfish tails
- 1 cup green onions, sliced
- ½ cup fresh parsley, chopped
- salt and black pepper to taste
- your favorite hot sauce
- steamed white rice

Directions

1. Heat a heavy 6 to 8 quart pot or cast-iron Dutch oven over medium heat.
2. Sauté Andouille to render and brown, 5-7 minutes.
3. Add okra and sauté for another 5-7 minutes.
4. Remove okra and Andouille, set aside.
5. Return pot to medium-high heat, add oil.
6. Whisk in flour, stirring constantly until dark brown roux is achieved, the color of dark chocolate, this may take a while.
7. Add the onions, celery, bell peppers and garlic. Sauté these vegetables until soft and translucent, 5-7 minutes.
8. Add stock gradually, stirring well to incorporate with the vegetables and roux.
9. Add the Andouille, okra and stir.
10. Cover, reduce heat, and simmer for 30 to 45 minutes, stirring occasionally.
11. Add crawfish tails, green onions, and parsley then stir, cover, simmer 5 more minutes.
12. Adjust salt, black pepper and hot sauce to taste.
13. Serve in a bowl over steamed white rice.

Abbeville Shrimp and Egg Gumbo

Ingredients

- ½ cup vegetable oil
- ½ cup all-purpose flour
- 1 onion, chopped
- 1 clove garlic, minced
- 4 cups hot water
- 2 cups chopped celery
- 1 bunch green onions, chopped
- 1 green bell pepper, chopped
- 1 red bell pepper, chopped
- 1 large tomato, chopped
- 1 bay leaf
- ½ teaspoon dried thyme
- 2 pounds shrimp, peeled and deveined
- 8 hard-cooked eggs
- 1 cup okra
- salt to taste
- ground black pepper to taste
- ¼ tablespoon cayenne pepper
- 3 cups cooked white rice

Directions

1. Heat oil in a Dutch oven or any heavy pan. Stir in flour to make a roux. Cook, stirring constantly, until roux is dark brown; be careful not to burn. Add onion and garlic, and cook until slightly wilted. Whisk in water.
2. Stir in celery, green onions, tomato, green and red peppers, okra, bay leaf, thyme, salt, pepper, and cayenne. Simmer for 1 hour.
3. Add shrimp and hard boiled eggs; simmer 15 to 20 minutes longer. Adjust seasoning to taste. Serve gumbo over rice.

Mon Mere's Gumbo

From Kellie Taylor-White

Ingredients

- 5 pounds 16-20 count shrimp
- 1 dozen blue crab (cleaned and split)
- 1 smoked turkey leg
- 1 dozen chicken wings
- 3 pounds of smoked sausage
- two bags of dried shrimp
- 2 pounds boneless smoked ham hocks
- 1½ onion (large)
- 1½ bell pepper
- 3 stalks of celery
- salt, pepper, sage (to taste)
- 3 bay leaves
- Tony Chachere's Creole seasoning (just because everything is good with Tony's in it)
- ½ jar of Zatarain's gumbo file'
- 1 cup of flour

Directions

1. Peel your shrimp and keep all heads and shells.
2. In separate pot, boil heads and shells to make a stock. At same time, in the pot you are going to make the gumbo in, begin boiling smoked turkey leg.
3. When shrimp stock is complete, add to turkey stock and continue cooking.
4. In non-stick frying pan, VERY CAREFULLY, brown flour with no oil.
5. If you do it with oil, your gumbo will be greasy and nobody likes greasy gumbo. Trust me everything else will give off grease, no need to add more.
6. DO NOT LEAVE your pan.
7. Flour scorches quickly so you have to stir constantly.
8. Put the flour aside.
9. Sauté finely chopped onions, celery and bell pepper (the trinity) in a little bit of olive oil.
10. When trinity is translucent, add flour, sage, salt, pepper, and a bit of Tony's to it
11. Add water until it looks like everything in your roux is good and fluid. "No big lumps not all watery either." That's what Mon Mere says.
12. Add this roux to your shrimp and turkey stocks.
13. Slice and render that sausage and ham in the same frying pan.
14. Add a little bit of olive oil if you need but drain off all that grease when you are done.

(Continued on Next Page...)

15. After you the grease is gone, you can add the meat to the gumbo.
16. Add bay leaf.
17. Throw in your chicken and file' now.
18. Bring to a boil and turn it down to medium heat.
19. Cook for about an hour.
20. Then, turn it down to low and throw in your crabs.
21. Cook for another hour.
22. Throw in the shrimp.
23. Cook until you are ready to eat or at least another half an hour.
24. Serve over rice.

Kellie says ... "this recipe serves at least twenty-five. Enough for Christmas and some left over for after all the company leaves. But you gotta set it aside before they come over or they will pick all your shrimp out."

Thanks Kellie!

Bunkie Chicken and Andouille Gumbo

Ingredients

- 1 cup dry roux
- 2 tablespoons of canola oil
- 2 cups onions, chopped
- 1 cup bell pepper, chopped
- 1 cup celery, chopped
- 1 fryer chicken, boiled, skinned and deboned
- ½ pound smoked chicken sausage, cut in ¼-inch rounds
- ½ pound andouille sausage, sliced
- 2 garlic cloves, chopped fine
- 2 chicken bouillon cubes
- ½ cup green onion, chopped
- ¼ cup parsley, chopped
- salt
- black pepper
- cayenne pepper to taste

Directions

1. Skin the chicken, add the bouillon cubes to a large pot of water and boil until done.
2. Remove the chicken and reserve the broth.
3. Let chicken cool, debone, and chop into small chunks.
4. In another large cast iron pot, over a medium flame, sauté the onions, peppers and celery in canola oil until the onions are clear

5. Add the smoked sausage and andouille and cook until brown.
6. Add the enough of the retained broth and the garlic to cover all Ingredients.
7. Bring to a boil and reduce to a simmer.
8. Mix the dry roux with one cup of water, whisking to be sure the roux is evenly wet then add this mixture to the skillet.
9. Now check the liquid, adding broth or hot water if needed. It should have the color of the roux and be just slightly thickened.
10. Simmer for about 30 minutes.
11. Add salt and black pepper to taste, then add ground red (cayenne) pepper -- enough to just to prick the tongue.
12. About 5- 10 minutes before removing from heat, add the green onion tops and parsley.
13. To serve, put a scoop of rice in your bowl and ladle on the gumbo.

You should have plenty of French bread to complete your meal, and then top it off with a good tossed salad.

Salades Satisfaisante

Arceneaux's Artichoke Salad

Ingredients

- 4 fresh artichoke hearts
- Salt to taste
- 1 tablespoon red wine vinegar
- 1 teaspoon worcestershire sauce
- 2 cans or jars of artichoke hearts, quartered
- 4 tablespoons olive oil
- 1 teaspoon slap ya mama hot sauce
- 1 tabl lemon or lime juice
- 1 large garlic clove

Directions

1. In a salad bowl, mash the garlic and salt.
2. Add the fresh artichoke hearts, and mash them with the garlic and salt.
3. Add your olive oil, stir, add lime juice, stir, add red wine vinegar, stir, now add the Slap Ya Mama, stir, add Worcestershire sauce, mix it good.
4. Place all your canned or jarred artichoke hearts in the dressing and let them marinate for 45 minutes, then eat over a bed of your favorite fresh salad greens.

Lake Martin Crawfish and Egg Salad

Ingredients

- 3 eggs, hard-boiled
- salt, to taste
- 1 tablespoon ranch dressing
- 2 tablespoons dill pickles, finely chopped
- 1 pound chopped crawfish or shrimp
- 1 teaspoon cayenne pepper
- 2 tablespoons mayonnaise
- 1 teaspoon Poupon mustard

Directions

1. To cook crawfish.
2. In a saucepan bring 2 quarts water to boil with 2 teaspoons salt and ½ teaspoon of red pepper.
3. Add peeled crawfish tails to water.
4. Bring to boil and remove from heat immediately.
5. Drain and cool.
6. Chop hard-boiled eggs.
7. Chop crawfish and mix with the eggs.
8. Add the pickles.
9. Mix mustard, Ranch dressing, and mayonnaise and add to Egg mixture.
10. Add additional pepper and salt to your liking

T-Coon's Cajun Potato Salad

Ingredients

- 2 pounds of red potatoes, cut into quarters, and peeled
- 2 teaspoons of salt
- 7 boiled eggs
- ¼ cup of olive oil
- 1 teaspoon of vinegar
- ¾ cup of mayonnaise
- 1 teaspoon (or more) of Slap Ya Mama hot sauce
- 1 chopped up sweet pickle
- 1 stalk of celery chopped up
- 1 small green bell pepper chopped up

Directions

1. Fill a pot half way with water and bring it to a boil.
2. Add your potatoes and salt and cook them for 5 minutes.
3. Drain the water out of the pot.
4. Add all ingredients to a bowl and mix it well.
5. Refrigerate for an hour or longer before serving.
6. Top off with some cayenne and paprika for color and flavor.

Fontenot's Fried Oyster Salad

Ingredients

- 2 12-ounce containers oysters, drained
- 2 eggs, beaten
- 1½ cups Italian seasoned breadcrumbs
- 1½ cups vegetable oil
- 5 large fresh mushrooms, sliced
- 1 10-ounce package fresh spinach
- raspberry vinaigrette
- 1 small onion, thinly sliced
- 5 slices bacon, cooked and crumbled

Directions

1. Dip oysters in egg whites; dredge in breadcrumbs.
2. Set aside.
3. Pour oil into a large heavy skillet; heat to 350°.
4. Fry oysters, until golden; drain on paper towels.
5. Arrange sliced mushrooms over spinach, and drizzle with half of Raspberry Vinaigrette.
6. Top with oysters, onion slices, and bacon, and serve with remaining vinaigrette.

Blanchard Beet Salad

Ingredients

- ½ pound Fresh beets
- ½ cup extra-virgin olive oil
- ¼ cup rice wine vinegar
- salt, to taste
- freshly ground black pepper, to taste
- 1 pound Crab meat; picked over
- ¼ cup reduced fat mayonnaise
- 2 tablespoons low fat sour cream
- 2 tablespoons minced shallots
- 1 tablespoon Prepared horseradish; or to taste
- ½ cup pickled red onions
- 1 tablespoon finely-chopped parsley

Directions

Prepare the Beets

1. Cut the tops and bottoms off the beets.
2. Place the beets in a small roasting pan and fill the pan with water coming ⅓ of the way up the pan.
3. Cover the pan with aluminum foil.
4. Place the pan in the oven and roast for about 30 to 35 minutes or until the beets are tender.
5. Cool slightly, about 20 minutes, and rub off the skin.
6. Using a mandoline, thinly slice the beets.
7. Reserve ¼ cup of the beet liquid.

8. In a mixing bowl, whisk the olive oil and rice wine vinegar together.
9. Season with salt and pepper.
10. Toss the beets with vinaigrette, cover and chill for 6 hours.

ASSEMBLE THE SALAD

1. In a mixing bowl, toss the crab meat, mayonnaise, sour cream, shallots and horseradish together.
2. Season the salad with salt and pepper.
3. To assemble, divide the beet slices into equal portions.
4. Cover the center of each plate with the beet slices.
5. Mound the crab salad over the beet slices on each plate.
6. Place pickled onions on top of each mound of crab salad.
7. Drizzle the reserved beet water around the edge of each plate. Garnish with parsley.

St. Mary's Strawberry Fields Forever Salad

Ingredients

- ¼ cup extra-virgin olive oil
- ¼ cup balsamic vinegar
- ¼ teaspoon dry mustard
- Salt and pepper
- 8 cups mixed salad greens
- 6 large Louisiana strawberries, hulled and sliced
- ½ cup chopped toasted pecans
- ½ cup thinly sliced red onion
- ½ cup crumbled unleaded blue cheese

Directions

1. In a small bowl, whisk together olive oil, vinegar, and dry mustard.
2. Add salt and pepper to taste.
3. In a large bowl, combine salad greens, strawberries, pecans, and red onion.
4. Toss with dressing.
5. Top with blue cheese and serve.

Bisques, Soups and Stews

Bertrand's Corn Bisque with Crabmeat

Ingredients

- 3 teaspoons olive oil
- 1 small onion (diced)
- 1 small jalapeno pepper (seeded and diced)
- 2 ears fresh corn (shuck kernels from cob)
- 1 cup low sodium chicken broth
- 3 cups water
- ¼ teaspoon salt
- fresh ground black pepper (to taste)
- ¼ cup 1% milk
- 1 tablespoon fresh oregano
- 8 ounces crabmeat (pasteurized, not canned) (remove shells carefully)
- 1 small shallot (minced)

Directions

1. Place 1 teaspoon olive oil in a large skillet over medium heat. Add the onion and jalapeno.
2. Cook, stirring well, for about 5 minutes and add the corn.
3. Cook for another 3 minutes and add the chicken stock, water, ⅛ teaspoon salt and the pepper.
4. Reduce the heat until the soup is simmering and cook for about 20 – 25 minutes until the corn is soft.
5. Let the soup cool slightly and then use a food processor or blender to puree in batches until smooth.
6. Force the pureed soup through a fine mesh sieve. Discard any of the solids from the sieve.
7. Return the soup to the pan and add the milk and oregano.
8. Reheat gently over low heat.
9. Let cook for about 10 minutes.
10. While the soup is heating, place the crabmeat in a bowl and add 2 teaspoons olive oil, ⅛ teaspoon salt and the minced shallot. Fold together.
11. When ready to serve, place the crab in the bottom of soup bowls and ladle soup into the bowl.

Vita's Vegetable Soup

Ingredients

- 6 cups chicken stock or water
- 3 medium tomatoes, peeled and chopped (about 1 ½ cups)
- 2 medium carrots, thinly sliced
- 1 medium onion, thinly sliced
- ½ medium green bell pepper, thinly sliced
- 1 10-ounce package frozen cut green beans
- 1 6-ounce can tomato paste
- 2 cups fresh broccoli florets
- 2 cups fresh cauliflower
- 1 cup frozen whole-kernel corn
- 1 teaspoon salt
- ½ teaspoon hot pepper sauce

Directions

1. In a 6-quart pot, combine all the ingredients and place over medium heat.
2. Cover and cook for 45 minutes, stirring occasionally.

Lafourche Parish White Bean Soup

Ingredients

- 1 ham bone
- 1 pound white beans
- 1 can whole tomatoes, mashed or chopped with juice
- 1 large onion, chopped
- 1 bell pepper, chopped
- ½ pound tasso, cubed
- 1 carrot, grated
- 3 medium red potatoes, peeled & cubed
- 5 cans chicken broth
- Red, black & white peppers to taste
- Tabasco to taste

Directions

1. Place all ingredients in soup kettle.
2. Bring to boil, lower heat and cover.
3. Simmer until beans and potatoes are "cooked to pieces", about 3 to 4 hours, stirring occasionally.
4. Remove ham bone.
5. Adjust seasonings to taste. Be sure to taste for salt before adding any...there's plenty in the tasso and chicken broth.

Terrebonne Oyster Soup

Ingredients

- 3 tablespoons butter
- 3 tablespoons all-purpose flour
- 1¼ cups chopped yellow onions
- 1 quart warm milk
- 4 dozen freshly shucked oysters, drained and oyster liquor reserved
- 3 tablespoons chopped fresh parsley leaves
- 3 tablespoons butter
- Salt and freshly ground black pepper to tas

Directions

1. Combine 3 tablespoons butter and the flour in a large, heavy pot over
2. medium heat.
3. Stirring slowly and constantly, cook for about 3 minutes.
4. Add the onions and cook, stirring, until soft, 3 to 4 minutes.
5. Combine the milk with the reserved oyster liquor and add slowly to
6. the roux mixture, stirring constantly. The mixture will thicken slightly.
7. Bring to a gentle boil, then reduce the heat to medium-low and
8. simmer for 2 minutes.
9. Add the oysters, parsley, 3 tablespoons butter and salt and pepper,
10. and simmer until the edges of the oysters curl.
11. Remove from the heat.
12. Serve warm with crackers or hot French bread.

Trahan Oyster and Artichoke Soup

Ingredients

- ½ cup butter
- 2 bunches green onions, chopped
- 3 ribs celery, chopped
- 3 cloves garlic, pressed
- 1¾ pounds fresh cut artichoke hearts or baby artichokes, or 3 9-ounce packages frozen artichokes hearts, defrosted and quartered
- 2 14-ounce cans artichoke hearts, washed, drained, and quartered
- 3 tablespoons flour
- 1½ quarts homemade chicken stock
- Cayenne to taste
- 1 teaspoon salt
- 1 tablespoon Worcestershire sauce
- ½ teaspoon fresh thyme
- 1 quart oysters, drained and chopped (reserve liquid)
- ⅓ cup sherry
- 1 cup heavy cream
- 1 cup milk

Directions

1. In a heavy 4-quart pot melt the butter over medium heat.
2. Add the green onion, celery, and garlic and sauté until soft.
3. Add the artichokes.
4. Sprinkle the mixture with the flour and stir to coat the vegetables well, but do not let the flour brown.
5. Gradually add the stock, stirring constantly.
6. Add the cayenne, salt, Worcestershire sauce, and thyme.
7. Simmer the mixture, covered, for 1 hour.
8. Add the oysters, oyster liquid, and sherry and simmer for 10 minutes.
9. Do not allow the soup to boil.
10. Stir in the cream and milk.
11. Cool and refrigerate for at least 8
12. hours.
13. Before serving, heat the soup slowly over low heat.

Cecelia Sweet Corn And Shrimp Soup

Ingredients

- 3 cups whole kernel corn
- 2 pounds freshwater (or other) shrimp
- 1 cup butter
- 1 cup chopped onions
- 1 cup chopped celery
- ½ cup chopped red bell pepper
- ½ cup chopped green bell pepper
- ¼ cup diced garlic
- 1 cup diced tomatoes, seeded
- 1 cup flour
- 1 cup tomato sauce
- 2½ quarts shellfish stock
- 1 cup heavy whipping cream
- ½ cup sliced green onions
- ½ cup chopped parsley
- Salt and cracked pepper to taste
- Tabasco to taste

Directions

1. In a two gallon stock pot, melt butter over medium high heat.
2. Add corn, onions, celery, bell peppers and garlic.
3. Sauté three to five minutes or until vegetables are wilted.
4. Add tomatoes, blend well into the vegetable mixture and add flour.
5. Using a wire whisk, whip constantly until a blonde roux is achieved.
6. Do not brown.
7. Add tomato sauce and stock, one ladle at a time, stirring constantly until all is incorporated. Bring to a low boil and reduce to simmer.
8. Add half of the shrimp and cook for thirty minutes.
9. Add remaining shrimp, cream, green onions and parsley.
10. Allow the shrimp to cook approximately ten minutes.
11. Season to taste using salt, pepper and favorite hot sauce.

Breaux Bridge Crawfish Stew

Ingredients

- 2 pounds cleaned crawfish tails
- ¼ cup tomato sauce
- 1 cup vegetable oil
- 3 quarts crawfish stock or water
- 1 cup flour
- 1 cup chopped green onions
- 2 cups chopped onions
- 1 cup chopped parsley
- 1 cup chopped celery
- Salt and cayenne pepper to taste
- 1 cup chopped bell pepper
- A dash or two of Tabasco
- 2 tablespoons diced garlic

Directions

1. In a two gallon pot, heat oil over medium high heat. Add flour and using a wire whisk, stir constantly until dark brown roux is achieved.
2. When brown, add onions, celery, bell pepper and garlic and sauté until vegetables are wilted,
3. approximately three to five minutes.
4. Add crawfish tails and cook until meat is pink and slightly curled.
5. Stir in tomato sauce and slowly add crawfish stock stirring constantly until all is incorporated. Bring to a low boil, reduce to simmer and cook thirty minutes, stirring occasionally.
6. Add green onions and parsley and season to taste using salt and pepper.
7. When done, serve over white rice with a few dashes your favorite hot sauce.

Kaplan Chicken Stew!

Ingredients

- 1 6-pound hen, cut up
- 1 tablespoon shortening
- 2 tablespoons all-purpose flour
- 3 onions, finely chopped
- 4 cups warm water
- Creole seasoning
- ¼ cup chopped green onions and parsley

Directions

1. In a Dutch oven, brown chicken in shortening; remove from pot.
2. Place flour in pot and stir until brown.
3. Add onions and cook until tender.
4. Add chicken and water.
5. Season with Creole seasoning.
6. Simmer for 1 hour.
7. During the last 5 minutes of cooking, add green onions and parsley.
8. Stir occasionally as stew thickens to prevent burning.
9. Serve over steamed rice.

Yields 6 servings.

Theriot Tomato Basil Soup

Ingredients

- 4 cups (8 to 10) tomatoes, peeled, cored and chopped
- 2 cups tomato juice
- 2 cups vegetable or chicken stock
- 14 washed fresh basil leaves
- 1 cup heavy cream
- ¼ pound sweet, unsalted butter
- Sea salt to taste
- ¼ teaspoon cracked black pepper
- 1 tablespoon fresh lemon juice
- 1 chicken bouillon cube
- 1 teaspoon olive oil

Direction

1. Combine tomatoes, juice, stock & bouillon in saucepan.
2. Simmer 30 minutes. Puree, along with the basil leaves, in small batches, in blender or food processor.
3. Return to saucepan and add cream, butter, olive oil and lemon juice while stirring, over low heat.
4. Garnish with basil leaves, add sea salt & cracked pepper to taste. (I also add a can of petite diced tomatoes!)
5. Serve with your favorite bread.

Accoutrements

Eunice Dirty Rice

Ingredients

- 2 tablespoons all-purpose flour
- 2 tablespoons vegetable oil
- 1 medium onion, chopped
- ½ medium green bell pepper, chopped
- 2 sticks celery, chopped
- ½ pound ground chuck
- ½ pound ground pork
- ½ pound ground chicken livers and gizzards
- 1 tablespoon salt
- ½ teaspoon paprika
- ⅛ teaspoon pepper
- ⅛ teaspoon garlic powder
- ½ teaspoon cayenne pepper or to taste
- 2 cups chicken stock or water
- 2 tablespoons cornstarch
- 1 bunch scallions, chopped
- 3 cups cooked rice, cooled

Directions

1. In a large heavy pot, make a roux by combining flour and oil and
2. stirring constantly over medium heat until dark brown in color. Be
3. careful not to burn.
4. Add onion, bell pepper and celery and cook until tender, about 20
5. minutes.
6. Add ground chuck, pork, chicken livers and gizzards and seasonings.
7. Brown, stirring occasionally, for about 30 minutes.
8. Add stock or water, cover and simmer for 2 hours over low heat.
9. Mix cornstarch with enough warm water to dissolve it.
10. Slowly add cornstarch mixture to pot.
11. Bring back to a boil; then turn fire off.
12. Add scallions and let cool.
13. When cooled, combine with rice.
14. At this point the dressing is complete.
15. If heating dressing in a casserole dish, bake at 375°F for 30 minutes.

Duplechain Dirty Rice

Ingredients

- 1 pound chicken gizzards -- finely chopped
- 1 teaspoon pepper
- 1 pound chicken livers -- finely chopped
- ⅛ teaspoon ground red pepper
- ¼ cup butter
- 3 cup hot cooked rice
- 1½ cup onion -- finely chopped
- ½ cup chopped parsley
- ½ cup celery -- finely chopped
- ¼ cup green pepper -- chopped
- 2 garlic cloves -- minced
- 2 teaspoon salt

Directions

1. Brown meat in margarine in large skillet.
2. Add onion, celery, green pepper, garlic and seasonings, mix well.
3. Cover.
4. Cook, stirring occasionally, over medium heat until vegetables are tender.
5. Add rice and parsley, mix lightly.
6. Serve immediately.

Mowata Couche Couche

Ingredients

- 2 cups of yellow cornmeal
- ¼ cups of vegetable oil
- 2 teaspoons of salt
- 1 teaspoon of baking powder
- ¾ cups of milk
- ¾ cups of water

Directions

1. In a heavy pot, heat the oil on high.
2. In a separate bowl, mix the cornmeal, salt, and baking powder.
3. To that bowl, add the milk and water and stir.
4. Pour the batter into the hot oil.
5. Allow the batter to form a crust on the bottom.
6. Reduce the heat to low and stir.
7. Cook for an additional 15 minutes, stirring occasionally.
8. Serve in a bowl with milk and sugar.

Trosclair Cornbread and Andouille Sausage Stuffing

Ingredients

- 4 tablespoons unsalted butter
- 1 cup andouille sausage, finely diced
- 1 cup spanish onion, finely diced
- 1 cup bell pepper, finely diced
- ½ cup celery, finely diced
- 2 tablespoons fresh garlic, mined
- 1 tablespoon fresh thyme leaves, chopped
- 1 tablespoon creole seasoning (less if using commercial, they have more salt)
- 4 cups leftover cornbread, crumbled
- ½ - 1 cup chicken stock
- 1 cup green onions, finely sliced
- 1 egg

Directions

1. Melt the butter in a large cast iron skillet over medium high heat, add the Andouille, cook until it starts to render .
2. Add the onion, bell pepper, celery, garlic, Thyme and Creole seasoning. Reduce the heat to medium.
3. Sweat the vegetable mixture until they are tender, stirring often.
4. Add the cornbread and stir well to coat with the Andouille and vegetable mixture. Reduce the heat to medium low.
5. Gradually add the stock until the mixture is moist.
6. Stir in the green onions, place the stuffing in a dish and cool in the refrigerator.
7. Once cool add the egg and mix well.

Chenevert Mirliton & Crawfish Casserole

Ingredients

- 4 medium mirlitons
- 2 tablespoons olive oil
- 1 cup chopped onions
- 1 cup chopped bell peppers
- 1 cup green onions
- 2 pounds crawfish tails
- 1 teaspoon thyme
- 2 tablespoons chopped garlic
- Salt and pepper
- 2 medium eggs, lightly beaten
- 1 cup Italian-style bread crumbs
- Grated Parmesan cheese

Directions

1. Cut mirlitons in half and remove seed but do not peel. Cut into 1-inch
2. dices and blanch in lightly salted water until tender and not overdone.
3. In olive oil, sauté onions, peppers and green onions; add diced mirliton
4. and crawfish. Blend well and cook for 10 minutes.
5. Stir in thyme, garlic, salt and pepper to taste.
6. Add eggs and bread crumbs slowly, adding only enough to absorb the liquid.
7. Mix well and put into a greased casserole dish.
8. Top with Parmesan and bake at 350°F for 30 minutes.

Cottonport Crawfish Casserole

Ingredients

- 1 pound louisiana crawfish tails
- 1 stick margarine
- 1 large onion
- 1 bundle of green onion
- 1-2 stalks celery
- ¼ bell pepper
- 4 cloves garlic
- ¼ teaspoon of cayenne pepper
- ¼ teaspoon black pepper
- 1 can of cream of mushroom or cream of shrimp soup
- 1 cup of bread crumbs

Directions

1. On medium fire, melt margarine in a 5 quart Dutch oven.
2. Add cut vegetables and sauté until onions start to clear and become soft - about 10 minutes.
3. Add crawfish tails and sauté an additional 5 minutes.
4. Take off heat and add cayenne, black pepper, cream of mushroom soup, and bread crumbs.
5. Mix well and put into casserole dish.
6. Bake at 350°F for about 30 minutes, uncovered.
7. Let stand 10 minutes before serving.
8. Serve with garlic bread and salad.
9. Serves about 5.

Latiolais Maque Choux

Ingredients

- 8 ears of fresh corn
- 1 chopped onion
- ½ chopped green bell pepper
- 1 stalk of celery, chopped
- 1 chopped green onion
- 1 cup of cubed salt meat
- 1 tablespoon of vegetable oil (or bacon grease if you can get it)
- 1 tomato chopped
- 2 teaspoons of salt
- 1 teaspoon of black pepper

Directions

1. Scrape the corn to remove the kernels
2. In a pot over medium heat, cook the onions and meat with the oil until they are lightly brown.
3. Add the celery and bell peppers to saute them.
4. Add the tomatoes and corn. Cover and let them simmer on a low heat for 30 minutes.
5. Add the green onions and the seasoning and let simmer, covered, for another 10 minutes.
6. Add some Cajun seasoning to taste.

Bourgeois Crawfish Pasta Casserole

Maude LeCompte Bourgeois

Ingredients

- ¼ cup olive oil
- 1 onion, chopped
- 1 green pepper, chopped
- 1 can Rotel
- ½ small can tomato sauce
- 1 teaspoon sugar
- 1 pound crawfish tails (preferably LA ones)
- 1 can cream of mushroom soup
- 8 ounces Velveeta cheese (I used Mexican mild)
- Water
- Salt
- 12 ounce package of angel hair spaghetti

Directions

1. Sauté onions and green peppers in olive oil until onions are clear.
2. Add can of Rotel, tomato sauce and 1 teaspoon of sugar.
3. Cook on medium heat for about 15 minutes. Stir as needed.
4. Add crawfish tails and 8 ounces Velveeta cheese. When cheese is
5. melted, take pot off of the fire.
6. While cooking the sauce, in another pot, put water to boil.
7. Once water is boiling, add 12 ounce package of angel hair spaghetti.
8. Boil until soft.
9. Once your spaghetti is boiled, put it in a casserole dish and mix well
10. with the crawfish sauce.
11. Place in 350°F oven for about 20 minutes.

Serves approximately 8-10

Cameron Mirliton Dressing

Ingredients

- 4 Mirlitons
- 1 onion, chopped or..
- 1 bunch green onions, chopped or both!
- 4-5 toes garlic, minced (or more)
- ½ cup chopped parsley
- ½ cup celery, and green pepper
- olive oil
- 1 cup Progresso Italian bread crumbs
- 1 cup freshly grated Romano cheese
- 1 pound of fresh shrimp, peeled and cut into pieces
- 2 teaspoons oregano, 4 teaspoons thyme, salt, pepper to taste and about 2-3 bay leaves

DIRECTIONS

1. Boil mirlitons whole until tender...but not mushy.
2. Peel, if necessary; remove seed in center and cut into cubes.
   Set aside.
3. Reserve boiling liquid
4. In a large pan, sauté vegetables in oil or margarine until limp; add shrimp.
5. Cook until shrimp are pink -- about one minute
6. Add chopped mirlitons with oregano, thyme, salt, pepper, and bay leaves.
7. Add bread crumbs (about ¾ cup).
8. Add 3/4 cup grated Romano cheese. Stir well.
9. Add liquid from boiling mirlitons to loosen.
10. Place in a greased casserole dish.
11. Sprinkle with ¼ cup bread crumbs, then ¼ cup grated cheese.
12. Dot with pieces of margarine.
13. Bake at 375°F until bubbly.
14. Brown top under broiler.

You may freeze it before or after baking.

Big Pete's Fried Cauliflower

Ingredients

- 1 large head cauliflower
- Tony Chachere's Creole Seasoning
- Whorchester Sauce
- Louisiana Green Tiger Sause
- Zatarains Seasoned Fish Fry with Lemon Flavor
- pure canola oil

DIRECTIONS

1. Wash cauliflower, removing excess green leaves and stalk.
2. Break or cut into small or large Florette's – make sure cauliflower is damp.
3. Lightly season with Tony Chachere's Creole Seasoning, Worchester Sauce & Louisiana Green Tiger Sauce.
4. In a gallon zip lock bag, pour ¼ of the bag full of Zatarains Seasoned Fish Fry with Lemon.
5. Shake several pieces at a time to coat well.
6. Fry in hot grease in batches until golden brown.
7. Drain well on paper towels.

I recommend using Pure Canola Oil.

This recipe can also be used to fry just about anything.

Peter Ducote

Atchafalaya Cheese Straws

Ingredients

- 1¼ cups quality cheddar (also good with gruyere, comté or beaufort) cheese
- ¾ cups flour
- ½ stick room temperature unsalted butter
- 1 large egg yolk, beaten
- ½ teaspoon cayenne
- Creole/Cajun seasoning to taste

Directions

1. Preheat the oven to 400°F.
2. Mix together the flour and cheese with your hands.
3. Work the butter in with your hands.
4. Add the egg yolk and seasonings and work in with your hands.
5. Knead the dough for a few minutes until it is a nice shiny ball.
6. Roll this out to a ⅓ inch thickness.
7. Cut into 2 inch strips and place on an ungreased cookie sheet.
8. Bake for about 15-20 minutes or until golden orange.
9. Let cool.
10. Store any remaining cheese straws in an airtight container.

Jennings Tomato Gravy

Ingredients

- ¼ cup bacon drippings
- 3 tablespoons all-purpose flour
- 2 cups water
- ½ 6-ounce can tomato paste
- salt and ground black pepper to taste

Directions

1. Heat bacon drippings in a skillet over medium-high heat.
2. Stir the flour into the bacon drippings and cook, stirring constantly, until lightly browned.
3. Slowly pour the water into the flour mixture while whisking.
4. Whisk in the tomato paste.
5. Cook the mixture until it begins to thicken.
6. Reduce heat to low and simmer until thick, about 5 minutes.
7. Season with salt and pepper.

A Lotta Lagniappe

(Lan-yap)

COCODRIE CRACKLIN

INGREDIENTS

- 1 pound of frozen pork skin
- some salt
- enough oil to fill a frying pot about half way
- some paper towels

DIRECTIONS

1. Heat the oil in a pot over medium-high heat.
2. Cut the pork skins into 1/2" pieces
3. Fry the pork skins in the pot until they are a golden brown (about 6 monutes)
4. Remove the pork skins and place them on the paper towels to drain.
5. Season with salt and Cajun/Creole seasoning

Seaux easy to make!

Parrain Pete's Boiled Cajun Peanuts

Ingredients

- 2 pounds of fresh and raw peanuts that are still in their shells
- 2 tablespoons of salt
- 1 bag of Zatarain's Crab and Shrimp Boil
- 1 tablespoon of red pepper or more or less to taste

Directions

1. Place the peanuts in a large pot and add enough water to cover them and almost fill the pot.
2. Add the salt and stir it real well.
3. Turn the stove to the high heat setting and cover until it boils.
4. Add the Zatarain's and the red pepper.
5. Reduce the heat just enough to keep it from boiling over.
6. Boil the peanuts for 4 hours. Add water as needed to keep the peanuts covered.
7. Drain the peanuts and serve.

New Iberia Crawfish Boudin

Ingredients

- 2 pounds crawfish tails
- 3 tablespoons cooking oil
- 4 large onions, chopped
- ⅛ cup flour
- ½ small can tomato sauce
- Salt, black and red pepper to taste
- 1 cup water
- 8 cups cooked rice
- Hog casing

Directions

1. Sauté crawfish tails in oil, stirring occasionally.
2. Add onions and let fry 5 minutes.
3. Add flour and mix well.
4. Pour in tomato sauce, salt, both peppers and let simmer for 5 minutes.
5. Add water and let cook about 25 minutes.
6. Add cooked rice and stuff into hog casing.
7. Drop in boiling water and simmer 10 minutes.

Ville Platte Seafood Linguine

Ingredients

- ½ cup olive oil
- ½ cup unsalted butter
- 1 large onion chopped
- 6 garlic cloves minced
- rosemary & oregano
- 28 ounce can tomatoes chopped
- salt & pepper
- 1 cup dry white wine
- ½ cup parsley
- cooked or raw shrimp, crab, lobster, scallops

Directions

1. In a skillet, heat butter and oil - sauté onion and garlic until golden.
2. Add wine; cook until liquid has evaporated and vegetables are golden.
3. Reduce heat; add tomatoes, spices, salt and pepper.
4. Add the seafood of your choice (scallops and raw shrimp take about 5
5. minutes to cook in sauce).
6. Fortuna's note: I like crab, shrimp and a can of lobster meat but basically any
7. combination works.

Landry Crawfish Etouffee

Ingredients

- 4 teaspoon Tabasco
- 1 small green bell pepper, chopped
- ⅓ cup vegetable oil
- ¼ cup flour
- 1 medium onion, chopped
- 2 cloves garlic, chopped fine
- 2 stalks celery, chopped
- 2 medium tomatoes, peeled and chopped
- 1 cup fish stock or Crawfish Water
- ½ teaspoon basil
- ¼ teaspoon thyme
- 1 bay leaf
- Freshly ground black pepper
- 1 pound crawfish, peeled
- ½ cup chopped green onions

Directions

1. Sauté the onions, garlic, celery, and bell pepper for about five minutes or until clear.
2. Add the tomatoes, stock, basil, thyme, and bay leaf.
3. Bring to a boil, stirring constantly.
4. Reduce the heat and simmer for fifteen minutes or until it thickens to a sauce.
5. Add the Tabasco, crawfish, green onions and simmer for an additional five minutes or until the crawfish/shrimp are cooked.
6. Remove the bay leaf and serve.

Charington Shrimp Creole

Ingredients

- ½ tablespoon olive oil
- 1 onion, finely chopped
- 3 bunches chives or 12 scallions, finely chopped (2 cups)
- 4 shallots, finely chopped
- 6 cloves garlic, finely chopped
- 1-2 chilies (very hot & fresh chilies), seeded and finely chopped
- 2 teaspoon finely chopped fresh ginger
- 1½ teaspoon curry powder
- 3 large ripe tomatoes, peeled, seeded and diced
- 1 cup finely chopped fresh parsley
- ¼ cup chopped fresh cilantro
- 1 teaspoon chopped fresh thyme or 1/4 teaspoon dried thyme leaves
- 1 bay leaf
- ⅓ cup dark rum
- 1 cup bottled clam juice
- 2 tablespoons tomato paste
- 24 jumbo shrimp, peeled and de-veined
- 2 tablespoons fresh lime juice
- ¼ teaspoon salt
- ¼ teaspoon freshly ground black pepper

Directions

1. Heat oil in a large nonstick skillet over medium heat.

2. Add onions, chives or scallions, shallots, all but 1 teaspoon of the garlic, chilies, ginger, and curry powder.
3. Cook, stirring, until just beginning to brown, 4-5 minutes.
4. Stir in tomatoes, 1/2 cup of the parsley, cilantro, thyme, and bay leaf.
5. Increase heat to high and cook, stirring, for 1 minute.
6. Stir in rum and bring to a boil.
7. Add clam juice and tomato paste.
8. Reduce heat and simmer until thickened and well-flavored, about 10 minutes. (The onion-tomato mixture can be made ahead to this point and kept covered in the refrigerator for up to 1 day. Return vegetable mixture to a simmer before proceeding.)
9. Meanwhile, place shrimp in a shallow glass dish and toss with 2 tablespoons lime juice, ¼ teaspoon salt, and ¼ teaspoon black pepper.
10. Cover with plastic wrap; refrigerate for 20 minutes.
11. Stir the marinated shrimp into the onion-tomato mixture.
12. Gently simmer over low heat, turning occasionally, until the shrimp are curled and opaque, 3-5 minutes.
13. Stir in the remaining 1 teaspoon garlic.
14. Taste and adjust seasonings with lime juice, salt, and pepper.
15. Sprinkle with the remaining ½ cup parsley and serve at once.

Opelousas Jambalaya

Ingredients

- 1 large frying chicken skinned and halved
- 1 pound smoke sausage thinly sliced
- 3 tablespoons olive oil
- ⅔ cup chopped green pepper
- 2 cloves garlic, minced
- ¾ cup chopped fresh parsley
- 1 cup chopped celery
- 1 28-ounce can tomatoes
- 2 cups chicken broth
- 1 cup chopped green onion
- 1½ teaspoon thyme
- 2 bay leaves
- 2 teaspoon oregano
- 1 tablespoon Creole seasoning
- ¼ teaspoon cayenne pepper
- ¼ teaspoon freshly ground pepper
- 2 cups raw long grain rice (Mahatma)
- 3 pounds medium raw shrimp or chicken meat
- 4 ounces tomatoes

Directions

1. In a 4 quart heavy pot, sauté sausage until firm and remove with slotted spoon.
2. Add olive oil to drippings and sauté green pepper, garlic, parsley and celery for 5 minutes. Chop tomatoes and reserve the liquid.

3. Add tomatoes, tomato liquid, chicken, chicken broth and green onion to the pot.
4. Stir in all spices.
5. Add the rice which has been washed and rinsed three times.
6. Add the sausage and cook for 30 minutes, covered, over low heat for about 7 minutes.
7. After most of the liquid has been absorbed by the rice, add the shrimp and cook until they turn pink. Transfer mixture to an oblong casserole dish and bake at 350 for approx 25 minutes.

Chicken Stock

1. Skin and cut chicken in half.
2. Clean insides and put in stock pot with enough water to cover an extra 2 inches or so.
3. Add 3 cloves garlic, 1 onion and two celery stalks.
4. Add salt/pepper to taste.
5. Cover until water comes to boil then uncover again.
6. Boil chicken for about 45 minutes or until done.
7. Take chicken out and continue boiling down stock until you are ready to use it.
8. Pull chicken off the bone, do NOT chop.
9. Set chicken aside until ready to use.

Gonzales Jambalaya

Ingredients

- One 3 to 4 pound hen cut into serving pieces
- 3 cups long grain rice - uncooked
- ¼ cup cooking oil
- 3 medium white onions - chopped fine
- 6 cups chicken stock
- 1 tablespoon salt, or to taste
- 2½ teaspoons granulated garlic
- 1 cup green onions - chopped
- ½ cup green peppers
- ½ cup celery - chopped fine
- ¼ teaspoon black pepper
- Red pepper to taste
- 2 tablespoons Louisiana hot sauce

DIRECTIONS

1. Fry chicken in cooking oil until golden brown.
2. Remove chicken and oil leaving just enough oil to cover bottom of pot.
3. Add onions, and fry until golden brown.
4. Put chicken back into pot with onions, and add 6 cups of water (note water level).
5. Add remaining seasoning and simmer covered until chicken is tender. If necessary, add enough water to bring back to previous level.
6. Bring back to a rolling boil, and add rice.
7. Simmer uncovered for about 15 minutes - turn rice.
8. Cover with tight fitting lid, let steam for 15 minutes, or until rice is tender.
9. Turn rice once more, and turn fire off.
10. Let stand for 10 minutes and then serve.

Jambalaya is tastier if highly seasoned, so don't forget the red pepper. When adding salt, water should taste a little too salty, as rice absorbs considerable salt.

Thibodaux Crawfish & Tasso Jambalaya

Jambalaya, like gumbo is another one of those classic, one-pot Louisiana meals heavily influenced by the Creoles and Cajuns. Its closest relative is the saffron scented and tinted paella found in Spanish cuisine. Because saffron wasn't exactly available on this side of the Atlantic, substitutions were made. Never yellow, the Creoles turned it red with the addition of tomatoes and seafood, while the Cajun versions were made brown with generous amounts of poultry, pork, and game. Also, like gumbo, there is no right or wrong, and it is the perfect dish to throw in any leftover or scraps of meat and vegetables.

Ingredients

- 3 tablespoons vegetable oil
- pound Tasso ham, diced
- cups onions, chopped
- ½ cup celery, chopped
- 1 cup red bell pepper, chopped
- 1 tablespoon garlic, minced
- 1 15-ounce can diced tomatoes
- cups white rice
- 6 cups chicken stock
- bay leaves
- 1 tablespoon Worcestershire sauce
- 2 teaspoons of your favorite Creole or Cajun seasoning

- 2 pounds Louisiana crawfish tails
- 1 cup green onions, sliced
- salt and black pepper to taste

Directions

1. Heat a heavy 6 to 8 quart stock pot or cast iron Dutch oven over medium heat.
2. Add oil and sauté Tasso until browned on all sides.
3. Add onions and sauté until brown and caramelized, 10 minutes.
4. Add celery, bell peppers, and garlic. Sauté these vegetables until soft and translucent, 5-7 minutes.
5. Stir in the tomatoes, rice and sauté for 2 minutes.
6. Add the stock, bay leaves, Worcestershire, and Creole or Cajun seasoning. Bring the liquid up to a boil, then cover, reduce heat, and simmer without stirring for 25 to 30 minutes.
7. When the rice is tender or all of the liquid has been absorbed, turn heat off
8. . Adjust salt, black pepper and hot sauce to taste
9. . Stir in the crawfish tails and green onions and cover.
10. Let the jambalaya rest for 10 minutes to allow the rice to fluff. Serve while hot.

Guidry's Deep-Fried Turkey

Ingredients

- 1 (approximately 14 pound) turkey
- 1 tablespoon Worcestershire sauce
- 2 tablespoons Creole mustard
- 3 2-ounce bottles garlic juice
- 3 2-ounce bottles onion juice
- 1 3 ounce bottle hot pepper sauce
- ¼ cup Creole seasoning
- 8 ounces water

Directions

1. Mix the following ingredients in a blender 2 days before cooking.
2. Pour into a jar and refrigerate.
3. Inject turkey with a syringe using the blended mixture.
4. Rub turkey with additional mustard and season generously with Creole seasoning.
5. When ready to cook, heat 5 gallons of peanut oil to 350 degrees; submerge turkey
6. and let fry for 4 minutes per pound of turkey.

Broussard Fried Oysters

Ingredients

- 24 large oysters, shucked
- 2 eggs
- ½ teaspoon salt
- ⅛ teaspoon pepper
- dash ground cayenne pepper, optional
- 2 tablespoons cold water
- 1 cup fine dry bread crumbs

Directions

1. Drain oysters.
2. Beat eggs with salt and pepper and cayenne.
3. Whisk in water.
4. Put bread crumbs in a shallow bowl.
5. Dip oysters, one at a time, into the egg mixture then into the bread crumbs.
6. Let rest for 5 minutes before frying.
7. Fry in hot deep fat at about 375°F until golden brown.
8. Serve immediately with cocktail sauce or tartar sauce, or use in sandwiches.

LeBlanc's Shrimp-Stuffed Mirlitons

Ingredients

- 4 mirlitons
- 1 tablespoon butter
- 1 cup finely chopped onion
- 2 garlic cloves, minced
- 2¼ cups cooked shrimp (about 14 ounces)
- ½ cup dry breadcrumbs
- 1 tablespoon chopped fresh parsley
- 1 teaspoon salt
- ¾ teaspoon hot sauce
- ½ teaspoon ground thyme
- 1 large egg, lightly beaten

Directions

1. Pierce mirlitons with a fork. Place in a Dutch oven; cover with water.
2. Bring to a boil over high heat; reduce heat, and simmer 30 minutes or until tender.
3. Drain and cool.
4. Cut mirlitons in half lengthwise; discard seeds. Scoop out pulp, leaving a 1/4-inch-thick shell.
5. Chop pulp and place in a large bowl.
6. Preheat oven to 375°.
7. Melt butter in a medium nonstick skillet over medium heat.
8. Add onion and garlic and cook 6 minutes or until onion is tender.
9. Add onion mixture, shrimp, and remaining ingredients to chopped pulp; stir to combine.
10. Spoon about 1/2 cup shrimp mixture into each shell.
11. Place stuffed mirlitons on a baking sheet. Bake at 375° for 30 minutes or until shrimp mixture is thoroughly heated and golden.

Jeansonne Crawfish Pie

Popularized by the Hank Williams song, "Jambalaya (On the Bayou)" Try it with different dough types such as short crust, flaky, puff, or phyllo varieties. Make them bite sized for appetizers or big enough for the whole family.

Ingredients

- Pre-made pastry dough (small preformed shells, large pie crust, or sheet pastry)
- 4 tablespoons butter
- 3 tablespoons flour
- small onion, diced
- stalks celery, diced
- 1 red bell pepper, diced
- cloves garlic, minced
- 1 15-ounce can diced tomatoes
- 1 tablespoon of your favorite Creole or Cajun seasoning
- 6 dashes of your favorite hot sauce
- 1 teaspoon Worcestershire sauce
- ½ cup heavy cream
- 1 pound Louisiana crawfish tails
- green onions, sliced
- ¼ cup fresh parsley, chopped
- salt and black pepper to taste

Directions

1. Follow any directions included with the pastry dough for optimum results in baking. Some frozen pastry types may require pre-cooking, or an egg wash. Otherwise, preheat the oven to 375°F.
2. Melt the butter in a large skillet over medium-high heat.
3. Whisk in flour, stirring constantly until light brown roux is achieved.
4. Add the onions, celery, bell peppers and garlic. Sauté these vegetables until soft and translucent, 5-7 minutes.
5. Add tomatoes, seasoning, hot sauce, Worcestershire, cream, and sauté 5 minutes or until sauce thickens.
6. Add crawfish tails, green onions, parsley, reduce heat, and simmer for 5 more minutes.
7. Remove from heat, fill pies or pastries, and bake for 20 to 30 minutes, or until crust is golden brown.
8. If using sheet dough, you will have to form into containing shapes and par cook before filling.
9. If desired, beat 1 egg and brush on pastry dough for a shiny glaze (yolk) and added crisp (white).

St. Amant Cajun Meatloaf

Ingredients

- 2 Whole bay leaves
- 1 tablespoon salt
- 1 teaspoon ground red pepper(cayenne)
- 1 teaspoon black pepper
- ½ teaspoon ground cumin
- ½ teaspoon ground nutmeg
- 4 tablespoons unsalted butter
- cup finely chopped celery
- ½ cup of celery finely chopped
- ½ cup finely chopped bell pepper
- ¼ cup chopped greens onions
- ½ teaspoon of minced garlic
- 1 tablespoon Tabasco sauce
- 1 tablespoon Worcestershire sauce
- ½ cup milk
- 2 pounds ground beef
- ½ pound of ground pork
- 2 eggs lightly beaten
- 1 cup very fine dry bread crumbs

Directions

1. Combine the seasoning mix ingredients in a small bowl and set aside.
2. Melt the butter in 1 quart saucepan over medium heat.
3. Add the onions, celery, bell pepper, green onions, garlic, Tabasco, Worcestershire and seasoning mix.
4. Sauté until mixture starts sticking excessively, about 6 minutes, stirring occasionally and scraping the pan bottom well.
5. Stir in the milk and ½ cup catsup.
6. Continue cooking for about 2 minutes, stirring occasionally.
7. Remove from the heat and allow mixture to cool to room temperature.
8. Place the ground beef and pork in an ungreased 13 x 9 inch baking pan.
9. Add the eggs, the cooked vegetable mixture removing the bay leaves, the bread crumbs.
10. Mix by hand until thoroughly combined in the center of the pan ... shape the mixture into a loaf that is about 1½ inches high x 6 inches wide and 12 inches long.
11. Bake uncovered at 350° for 25 minutes, then raise heat to 400°F and continue cooking until done, about 35 minutes longer.
12. Serve immediately,

Big Peter's Boiled Crawfish

(A great version of this classic south Louisiana specialty!)

Ingredients

- 1 sack of live crawfish
- ½ pot or less water
- ¼ of 2.5 ounce bottle of the following spices: garlic power, onion power & oregano
- ½ of 14 ounce bag Zatarian's Pro Boil*
- ½ of 16 ounce bag Louisiana Crawfish Boil
- 1 stick margarine
- 5 or 6 oranges – quartered
- 12 red potatoes cut in half
- 12 ears of sweet corn

Directions

1. Clean crawfish thoroughly – purge** if desired. In large pot, add water.
2. Add seasonings & spices to pot with water boiling (more or less to desired taste).
3. Squeeze and add quartered oranges to pot.
4. Add stick of margarine*** and halved potatoes and corn.
5. Boil potatoes until slightly tender.
6. Add sack of crawfish – water will cool down.
7. Let water come back to a boil then turn off fire & let soak for approximately 30 minutes depending on size & texture of crawfish.
8. While soaking crawfish, either leave lid on or off to control cooking time,

9. You must taste test regularly during this process to determine if they're ready.
10. Drain liquid from pot, or if using basket, lift out & spread crawfish on prepared picnic table and feast out!

Of course, while boiling & eating crawfish, make sure you have the
right beverage near, an ice cold beer!

*For milder and different flavor, you may substitute ¾ of 17 oz. can of Tony Chachere's Creole Seasoning and ¼ box of salt if needed instead, of Pro Boil and La. Crawfish Boil.

**Purging – means pouring ½ box salt over crawfish while cleaning to get the
muddy taste out of crawfish. This process cleans the crawfish to have a better
flavor.

***Adding the margarine makes the crawfish come out of the tail easier and whole, instead of breaking.

The City of Bunkie hosts the annual Louisiana Corn Festival every year, the 2nd full weekend in June.

Recipe courtesy of Peter Ducote

Clotilde's Cajun Cornish Hens

Ingredients

Cajun Rub

- ¼ teaspoon cayenne pepper
- 1 teaspoon seasoned salt
- 1 teaspoon garlic powder
- 4 Cornish hens
- 1 teaspoon onion powder
- 2 tablespoon olive oil
- 1 teaspoon dried thyme, crushed
- 1 teaspoon dried oregano, crushed
- ½ teaspoon paprika
- ½ teaspoon pepper

Directions

1. Preheat oven to 400°F.
2. Blend the Rub ingredients in a small bowl.
3. Wash and dry the Cornish hens.
4. Brush the hens with olive oil. Season the hens with the Cajun Seasoning.
5. Place the hens in a baking pan and let stand for about 5 minutes.
6. Bake hens about 45 to 60 minutes.

Lacassine Peppered Shrimp

Ingredients

- 1 pound butter
- ½ cup lime juice
- 2 teaspoons fresh basil, chopped
- 2 teaspoons cayenne pepper
- 2 teaspoons fresh oregano, chopped
- 6 garlic cloves, minced
- 1 bay leaf, crumbled
- ½ cup black pepper, finely ground
- salt to taste
- 4 pounds jumbo raw shrimp in shells

Directions

1. Melt the Butter in a large deep-sided frying pan or iron skillet over low heat.
2. When melted, raise the heat, and add the remaining ingredients except for shrimp.
3. Cook, stirring often, until browned to a rich mahogany color, about 10 minutes.
4. Add the shrimp, stir well to coat with the cayenne butter.
5. Cook until the shrimp have turned a rich deep pink, about 9 to 12 minutes.
6. Serve shrimp in shells, peel at table.

Lake Charles Cajun Pizza

Ingredients

- 1 8-ounce can tomato sauce
- 1 teaspoon dried oregano
- ½ teaspoon dried basil
- ½ teaspoon salt
- ¼ teaspoon garlic powder
- ⅛ teaspoon pepper
- 4 drops red pepper sauce
- 2 cups Bisquick® baking mix
- ½ cup cold water
- ½ cup shredded Monterey Jack cheese
- ⅓ cup chopped green pepper
- ⅓ cup chopped onion
- 1 10-ounce package frozen sliced okra, thawed, drained
- 1½ cups frozen peeled medium shrimp, thawed
- 1 tomato, seeded and chopped
- 1 cup shredded mozzarella cheese

Directions

1. Heat oven to 425°F.
2. Combine tomato sauce with oregano, basil, salt, garlic powder, pepper, and hot pepper sauce.
3. Mix baking mix and the cold water.
4. Roll into 12-inch circle on cookie sheet; pinch edge, forming ½ inch rim.
5. Spread with pizza sauce.
6. Sprinkle shredded Monterrey Jack cheese over crust.
7. Top with pepper, onion, okra, shrimp and chopped tomato.
8. Sprinkle with the shredded mozzarella cheese.
9. Bake until crust is golden brown, 20 to 25 minutes.

La Dent Sucree

Rayne Strawberries and Cream Bread Pudding

Ingredients

- 2 tablespoons butter, melted
- 7 slices day-old bread, torn into small pieces
- ¾ cup chopped fresh strawberries
- 3 eggs
- 1¼ cups milk
- ¾ cup light cream
- ¼ cup strawberry preserves
- ¾ cup white sugar, or to taste
- 1 teaspoon vanilla extract

Directions

1. Preheat oven to 350°F.
2. Butter the bottom and sides of an 8 inch square baking dish with the melted butter.
3. Toss bread with the chopped strawberries, and place into the prepared pan.
4. Beat the eggs, milk, cream, strawberry preserves, sugar, and vanilla in a medium bowl until frothy.
5. Pour over the bread and lightly press down with a spatula until the bread has absorbed the milk mixture.
6. Bake in the preheated oven for 40 to 45 minutes, or until the top springs back when lightly tapped.

Baleu's Banana Nut Muffins

Ingredients

- 3 bananas
- 1 cup all-purpose flour
- ½ cup sugar
- 1 cup whole wheat flour
- ½ cup brown sugar
- 1½ teaspoons baking soda
- 2 eggs
- 3 tablespoons buttermilk
- ½ cup butter, melted
- ¼ cup walnuts, chopped

Directions

1. Preheat oven to 300°F.
2. Spray 12-muffin tin with no-stick cooking spray.
3. Mash bananas in a medium mixing bowl.
4. Add sugar, brown sugar and eggs.
5. Mix well.
6. Add butter.
7. Stir in flour, whole wheat flour and soda.
8. Add buttermilk and walnuts.
9. Mix until just moistened.
10. Spoon into muffin tin.
11. Bake until muffins are brown and done, about 20 minutes.

Assumption Parish Beignets

Ingredients

- 1½ cups of warm water
- 1 envelope of active dry yeast
- ½ cup of regular sugar
- 1½ teaspoons of salt
- 2 eggs that are beaten
- 1 cup of evaporated milk
- 7 cups of flour
- ¼ cups of softened shortening
- enough oil to fill your pot up to about 3" deep, at least
- a bag or box of powdered sugar

Directions

1. Sprinkle the yeast over the warm water in a large bowl.
2. Stir the yeast and water and let it sit for 5 minutes.
3. Add the salt, sugar, eggs, and evaporated milk. Blend them really well with a whisk.
4. Add about 4 cups of the flour and blend until it is smooth.
5. Add the shortening, and then slowly add the rest of the flour while you are blending.
6. Cover the mixture with plastic and chill it overnight.
7. Roll the mixture onto a floured board until it is about 1/8" thick.
8. Cut it into 3" squares.
9. Fry each of the beignets until they are a golden brown on each side.
10. Pour powdered sugar over them and serve.

Louisiana Watermelon Cake

Ingredients

- 1 package *(18-¼ ounces) white cake mix*
- 1 package *(3 ounces) watermelon gelatin*
- 1¼ cups *water*
- 2 eggs
- ¼ cup canola oil
- 2½ cups prepared vanilla or cream cheese frosting, divided
- red and green gel food coloring
- hocolate chips

Directions

1. In a large bowl, combine the cake mix, gelatin, water, eggs and oil; beat on low speed for 30 seconds.
2. Beat on medium for 2 minutes.
3. Pour into two greased and floured 9-in. round baking pans.
4. Bake at 350°F for 30-35 minutes or until a toothpick inserted near the center comes out clean.
5. Cool for 10 minutes before removing from pans to wire racks to cool completely.
6. Set aside 2 tablespoons frosting for decorating.
7. Place 1¼ cups frosting in a bowl; tint red.
8. Tint remaining frosting green.

9. Place one cake layer on a serving plate; spread with ½ cup red frosting to within ¼ inch of edges.
10. Top with second cake.
11. Frost top with remaining red frosting to within ¾ inch of edges.
12. Frost sides and top edge of cake with green frosting.
13. Cut a ¼ inch hole in the corner of pastry or plastic bag.
14. Fill the bag with reserved white frosting. Pipe around top edge of cake where green and pink frosting meets.
15. For seeds, insert chocolate chips upside down into cake top.

Granier Red velvet cupcakes

Ingredients

- 2 cups cake flour
- 2 teaspoons baking powder
- ¼ teaspoon baking soda
- ½ teaspoon kosher salt
- ¾ cup buttermilk
- 2 tablespoons red food coloring
- ½ cup (1 stick) unsalted butter, at room temp
- 1 cup plus 2 tablespoons granulated sugar
- 2 large eggs, at room temp
- ½ teaspoon vanilla
- cream cheese frosting
- chocolate syrup or chocolate fudge sauce, optional

Directions

1. Preheat the oven to 325°F.
2. Sift together flour, baking powder and baking soda.
3. Add the kosher salt after sifting and set aside.
4. Measure out the buttermilk and red food coloring.
5. Add the die to the buttermilk for easier incorporation later.

6. Cream the butter and the sugar using an electric mixer, until the mixture is pale and fluffy.
7. Add the eggs one at a time, letting the eggs beat for 1 minute in between additions.
8. Scrape down the bowl in between additions.
9. Add the dry ingredients alternately with the wet ingredients.
10. Start by adding one third of the flour mixture. Mix just to incorporate.
11. Add half of the buttermilk.
12. Add another one third of the flour mixture.
13. Mix to incorporate. Add the last half of buttermilk, followed by the last third of flour.
14. Spoon into paper lined cupcake pans (makes 12).
15. Check the cupcakes for done-ness after 12 minutes.
16. Let cool completely before topping with cream cheese frosting, and a drizzle of chocolate sauce.

St. Martinville Peach Cobbler

Ingredients

- ½ cup butter
- 1 cup flour
- 1½ teaspoons baking powder
- ½ teaspoon salt
- 1 cup sugar
- 1 cup milk
- 3 cups peeled & sliced fresh peaches with their juices
- 1 teaspoon lemon juice

DIRECTIONS

1. Preheat oven to 350°F.
2. Peel and slice peaches.
3. Place into a glass bowl.
4. Add the lemon juice.
5. Stir gently.
6. Put the butter in a 9" x 13" glass baking dish, and put dish in preheated oven.
7. While the butter is melting, mix up the batter by combining the flour, baking powder, salt, sugar and milk.
8. When the butter is completely melted, remove the pan and pour the batter into the melted butter.
9. Then carefully spoon the peaches and juice evenly over the batter.
10. Return dish to the oven and bake for 30 minutes.
11. As the cobbler cooks, the batter will rise up and around the peaches.

LA Louisiane Smooth Pecan Pralines

Ingredients

- 2 cups sugar
- ½ cup cane syrup
- ½ cup water
- 2 cups pecan halves
- ½ stick butter
- 1 tablespoon vanilla

Directions

1. In a heavy 3 qt saucepan, combine sugar, cane syrup, water and pecans.
2. Stir over medium heat until sugar is dissolved, and mixture comes to a boil.
3. Cook, stirring occasionally, until mixture reaches "soft ball" stage (a small amount forms a soft ball when dropped into cold water).
4. Remove saucepan from heat, add butter and vanilla.
5. Allow candy to cool.
6. Whip until mixture gradually changes to lighter color and becomes creamy.
7. Drop by tablespoon on buttered cookie sheet. Push mixture from tablespoon with a teaspoon to hasten dropping before praline becomes too firm to shape.

Purgatory Pie

Ingredients

- ½ cup chopped fig preserves
- 1 tablespoon vanilla
- 1 cup chopped pecans
- 3 eggs, beaten
- ½ cup sugar
- pinch of cinnamon
- 1 tablespoon corn starch
- pinch of nutmeg
- 1 cup Karo syrup
- 1 9-inch uncooked pie shell
- ¼ cup Louisiana cane syrup

Directions

1. Preheat oven to 325°F.
2. In a large mixing bowl, combine sugar and corn starch.
3. Add syrups, vanilla, and eggs.
4. Using a wire whisk, blend thoroughly.
5. Add chopped pecans and fig preserves and blend well into the mixture.
6. Season with a pinch of cinnamon and nutmeg.
7. Pour ingredients into pie shell and bake on the center rack of oven for 45 minutes.

About the Author

Todd-Michael St. Pierre, has developed recipes for Cooking Light Magazine; his books have been featured in The Denver Post, The San Francisco Chronicle, The Baton Rouge Advocate, The Lafayette Advertiser, and AOL Food.

You can read more about the author and his books at www.ToddStPierre.com

Partial list of books by Todd-Michael St. Pierre

Children's titles:

- Fat Tuesday: LA Chatte Noire
- New Orleans Night Before Christmas
- Makin' Groceries
- Nola and Roux: The Creole Mouse & The Cajun Mouse
- The Crawfish Family Band
- Thibodeaux Turtle and Boudreaux Bunny
- Thunderful
- My Dream: A Vision of Peace
- Who Taught Time to Fly
- A Place Called Morning

Cookbooks:

- ⚜ Jambalaya, Crawfish Pie, Filé Gumbo: Cajun & Creole Cuisine
- ⚜ A Streetcar Named Delicious: I Love New Orleans Cookbook
- ⚜ Who Dat Cookin': The SAINTly & Sinful Flavors of South Louisiana
- ⚜ A Confederacy of Scrumptious: Weird & Wonderful New Orleans Cuisine
- ⚜ True Blood Cuisine: The Vampire Cookbook
- ⚜ The French Quarter Cookbook: Delectable New Orleans
- ⚜ Best of the Big Easy: Savoring New Orleans
- ⚜ Geaux Purple and Gold: Louisiana Tailgating Cookbook
- ⚜ The Mardi Gras Cookbook: New Orleans Carnival Cuisine
- ⚜ House of the Rising Bun: Baking New Orleans

Made in the USA
San Bernardino, CA
23 November 2013